MW00851713

The California Casa

RIZZOLI
NEW YORK

New York · Paris · London · Milan

The California Casa

DOUGLAS WOODS

Photography by MELBA LEVICK

Introduction by M. BRIAN TICHENOR

First published in the United States of America in 2012 by
RIZZOLI INTERNATIONAL PUBLICATIONS, INC.
300 Park Avenue South, New York, NY 10010
www.rizzoliusa.com

ISBN-13: 978-0-8478-3849-3
Library of Congress Control Number: 2011941747

© 2012 Rizzoli International Publications, Inc.
Text (except as noted below) © 2012 Douglas Woods
Introduction © 2012 M. Brian Tichenor
Photography © 2012 Melba Levick

Distributed to the U.S. Trade by Random House, New York

Page 1: *A collection of California pottery, including Bauer and
Gladding McBean pieces on the stoop of the Burnham House,
Capo di Monte, Hollywoodland (p. 140)*
Pages 2–3: *Entrance to the Chimorro House, Beverly Hills (p. 148)*

Designed by Abigail Sturges

Printed and bound in China

2015 2016 2017 2018 2019 / 10 9 8 7 6 5 4 3

Contents

Preface

Garden at the Christiancy Estate in Rancho Santa Fe (p. 38)

What began in America as a simple form of architecture built under the direction of the Spanish missionaries, the ingenious whitewashed adobe missions of Alta California became the lasting inspiration for a quintessential residential style beloved the world over.

Southern California, with its enviable Mediterranean climate, embraced the thick walls and shaded corridors as a means to shelter from the dry heat of the summer and occasional heavy rains of the winter. The Spanish Revival style is rooted in the mission precedent, but, as demonstrated by the selection of houses in this book, it has also been stretched in every possible direction by dreamers hoping to somehow emulate the Old World while marrying it to their day.

Many of the architects of California's golden age employed the Spanish style in the years between the world wars to make wonderful architecture. From small bungalows and courtyard apartments to huge mansions, they demonstrated that the Spanish Revival style worked well at any scale. As our best examples of this revival near 100 years of age, more people than ever are coming to appreciate that the Spanish invented the perfect house for this perfect environment.

While the homes in this book may not yet qualify as truly historic compared to their Spanish Mediterranean ancestors, some are certainly landmarks. Such is the case with George Washington Smith's Casa del Herrero, which serves as the main template for pioneered multi-unit courtyard housing in Los Angeles, and the amazing La Casa de las Campanas, designed by Lester Scherer and his visionary young client Lucile Mead which still dares anyone to try to do better.

Introduction

M. Brian Tichenor

Framed view of the Hollywood reservoir from the Longan Estate, Castillo del Lago (p. 128)

In the wave of development that has characterized Southern California in the years since the Second World War, it is sometimes difficult to see how unique and influential the region has been for that quintessential twentieth-century building type: the single-family house. A rare confluence of events combined, in what had initially seemed like the far end of the great American desert, to create a land of unlimited economic and cultural promise. Agriculture, oil, and motion pictures were the combined engines that focused the nation's attention to its furthest southwest corner and drew a flood of new residents. In American history before this, there had never been such a mass migration, and into a landscape and climate that was inherently different from the rest of the country. This region, with very little in the way of a true aesthetic heritage, was a virtual *tabula rasa*.

That the same houses that these immigrants were accustomed to in the eastern states would be less than ideal for their new environs was clear from the start: but what to build instead?

Intriguingly, in the late nineteenth century, a myth began to emerge, a romantic dream of an imagined past for Southern California, populated by exotic characters in a kind of new Eden, with vine-covered adobes nestled in luxuriant, sunny landscapes. This vision was fueled in no small part by a tourist industry based on the popular novel *Ramona*, which persuasively painted a picture of a land of promise with a languorous past wholly different from any other history that had transpired within the borders of the United States. It hardly mattered that little of the tale was true. The newcomers' enthusiasm for a Mission Style, based on the scant relics of Franciscan colonization, was the first attempt at a regional expression. But the kit of architectural parts used in the early adobes was limited: heavy, dark, and with little

adornment. Though this narrow vocabulary was suitable, in some cases, for public buildings, it did not translate well to the emerging requirements of the suburban middle class house. But the desire to integrate a sense of exoticism, that of a tangible past, had become a part of southern California's nascent identity.

The beginning of the twentieth century saw an inventive flowering of the Bungalow Style, which, in a curious combination of Japanese house and Swiss chalet, proliferated on acres of new houses infused with a comfortable Craftsman aesthetic, and which set the pattern for future suburban development in Southern California. And yet, with the romantic Latin overlay of a mostly imagined past, a fecund Mediterranean climate, and a burgeoning regional identity, a broader synthesis was to be made. As historian David S. Gebhard observed in his volume *George Washington Smith 1876–1930: The Spanish Colonial Revival in California*, the Spanish Colonial Revival and the less academic Mediterranean Revival styles constitute the only examples in American architectural history where by essentially popular consensus, a regional style was adopted. And, as is apparent in the images in this book, much of its success was due to both the populism and the accommodating inclusiveness that could be viably expressed in this romantic hybrid style.

The story of this period often features an influx of East Coast Brahmins-of-Industry, fresh from their grand European touring, settling, for their health and leisure, in one of several moneyed enclaves. These industrialists brought their erudition and good breeding to bear on great houses, rendered in refined European styles, effecting a kind of aesthetic trickle-down mechanism that was brought to bear upon the wider culture. This is only part of the story, though, and, by itself, does not explain a popular move-

ment. While there was a plethora of brilliant pattern books, yielding meticulous, well-studied examples of historic precedent from the buildings of the western Mediterranean, and astonishingly adventurous wealthy clients to build great houses with great architects, these buildings were but expressions of a much broader, popular enthusiasm. This early twentieth century period is characterized by a refreshingly non-pedantic sense of architectural freedom, which is perhaps why it was so much more successful than the more parochial Mission Revival style. How much of the development of this new regional architecture is inherently due to the new requirements of twentieth century living, to the great desire to take advantage of the possibility of outdoor living, or to the somewhat mad set designs of the great motion picture studios of Hollywood, is hard to discern from the distance of ninety years. What we do know is that a kind of Golden Age of residential design emerged and subsequently informed everything that followed, from expansive manors to humble courtyard apartments.

While several architects were well on the way to defining this new regional style in Southern California, one cannot overstate the influence of the great New York architect Bertram Goodhue in the creation of the stylistic synthesis that fostered this rising tide of free historicism. In the designs of both houses and gardens, and with the tremendously influential urban setting of the Panama-California Exposition of 1915, Goodhue's vision for a regional style for Southern California would prove, multiple times, the rallying statement for the nascent Spanish Colonial Revival movement. His El Fuerdis in Montecito ignited the fashion for grand Mediterranean houses, and, of equal importance, their structured, axial gardens. His Días Felices estate,

later named Val Verde, became the highly influential magnum opus of the great garden designer and bon vivant Lockwood de Forest. Most importantly, Goodhue's revolutionary amalgam of styles in the "Spanish Village" of San Diego's Panama-California Exposition would emerge as the stylistic bellwether on which the rapidly growing Southern California, then emerging from the end of the First World War, would base its regional architectural identity. This book features new photographs of Goodhue's Coppell Mansion in Pasadena, an impressive example of his residential style, albeit with the curious distinction of being a restoration of but one-half of the original building, the other having been calved off in a 1950s subdivision of the larger property.

Goodhue's eclectic lead was expanded upon by a new generation of extraordinary architects in the post-WWI period. Some, such as George Washington Smith in Santa Barbara, would take their firsthand knowledge of European architecture, bolstered by extensive travels on the continent, to create a coherent, flexible language, which, while fluent in attributable historical detail, responded with ease and sureness to the new requirements of the modern American single-family home. Others, like Stiles Clements in Los Angeles, would apply the exuberant showmanship learned from their experience designing movie palaces to free-wheeling, dazzlingly inventive essays in a new style, in which the Spanish style was only the starting point.

Looking at the press from these years shows us that there was great public interest in these developments. There were public workshops in Santa Barbara exploring the urban design possibilities of this developing regional style, movie stars were pictured in their new homes, and newspapers sponsored showcase houses showing just how perfect life could be in one's own California *hacienda*. The ever-expanding array of architectural possibilities in this new Southern California style was being rapidly assimilated into the fabric of the cities and suburbs throughout the region. It is fascinating to observe how accomplished and inviting the

smaller houses and apartments in this book are: that one could rent an apartment in as beautiful a building as the Andalusia, and share as fully in the languid romanticism of the time as the owner of an estate might, is testament to the power of this populist dream.

The inherent breadth of aesthetic inclusiveness can be seen in the way these disparate stylistic expressions could be plausibly integrated into a single Mediterranean Revival–style house. This tendency is seen in the Overell Estate in La Canada Flintridge, where an Art Deco facade finds an unexpected but compelling home in a more familiar arched arcade. This kind of flexibility of style is perhaps what speaks to us still: there is a strangely democratic expressiveness in the homes of this period, where everything from the most perfect historically modeled facade to the most exuberant unstudied confection could be arguably part of a consistent, if not entirely coherent, stylistic movement.

That this dream of a white-washed home in its own sunny garden began with a prominent component of land ownership and of newly realized aspirations to both outdoor living and decorative gardening are attributes that make these buildings so significant for the future of suburban housing in America. It is from these roots that the ranch house sprang. Its first great author, the sixth-generation San Diegan Cliff May, drew heavily from both the heritage and the fictions of the day to create his prototypical, and in their early ranch-house versions, very Spanish, populist homes. An interesting example in this book clearly illustrates the forces at play in this movement: a beautiful courtyard *rancheria*, the Christiancy Estate, in San Diego County, which carries all the aspirations of the time. Its architect, Lillian Rice, in addition to being one of the handful of extremely influential, first-generation Californian women architects, was a veteran of Richard Requa's office and had traveled under those auspices to Spain to work on his iconic pattern book *Old World Inspiration for American Architecture*. (This work was published by the Portland Cement company, so vital was the promulgation of the stucco styles to their

Rosson House garden courtyard (p. 208)

business.) Her legacy, as exemplified by this house, became the guiding light for the community of Rancho Santa Fe, a seminal early planned community that melded the agrarian dreams of suburban living with Rice's own very sophisticated aesthetic synthesis of Spanish rural architecture and the emerging indoor-outdoor living paradigm. Her self-coined lexicon of "Spanish-isms" became the stylistic vocabulary of the town and its highly cohesive enclave, much as George Washington Smith's work had informed the rebuilding of Santa Barbara after the disastrous 1925 earthquake there.

Much has been seen in books and publications of the houses of the wealthy in the Mediterranean Revival style; what is more poignant and indicative of the populist thrust of this new regional movement are the modest houses, several of which are documented in these pages. In the Rufus Keeler House, dazzling encrustations of tile on so many surfaces speak to the continued importance of the California craftsman tradition at all levels of society and of the widespread appeal that "Spanish" iconography held. The density of period decorative artifacts, which we see collected in many of these houses, also indicates just how popular and pervasive the accouterments associated with this immersive lifestyle were. The gardens, too, speak to a new and compelling tradition that would characterize Californian houses from this period forward: where the exuberance of the first "Southland" landscapes showed the near unimaginable wealth of horticultural possibility inherent to the region, the Spanish-style gardens of the 1920s and 30s introduced both the pleasures of a truly indoor-outdoor lifestyle and the compelling rigors of the Mediterranean "outdoor room," with its fountains and rills, tile works, and formal, yet habitable, courtyard plans.

So, in looking at the extraordinary houses in this book, the reader can consider just how unique and compelling was the shared dream of the faraway and the exotic that generated them, and how inspiring the houses continue to be. The integration of this eclectic visual language with the many varied desires of the individuals who created them created a rich moment in American architectural history—a strange, Golden Age indeed.

The Hollywood sign caps the hilltop overlooking Hollywoodland

Left: Looking into the foyer through iron gates

Right: The reconfigured main entry to the Coppell Mansion

Following pages: Left: Living room ceiling detail

Right: The former dining room, now the living room

Coppell Mansion

Pasadena, 1915
Bertram Goodhue, architect

The partnership of Bertram Goodhue and Carleton Winslow did not just produce the influential architecture of the 1915 Panama-California Exposition in San Diego. The pair are responsible for, among other great buildings and churches, the Los Angeles Public Library and the Griffith Observatory, both landmark civic gems that have one foot in the colonial past and the other in the optimistic present expressed in their Art Deco–style designs. Both Goodhue and Winslow completed impressive residential commissions at the time as well.

Taken by the designs they saw at the 1915 Panama-California Exposition, New York couple Herbert and Georgia Coppell commissioned Goodhue to design a country home to

14

*The living room
walk-in fireplace
accented with old
Spanish tile*

18

*Previous pages:
KAA Architects
re-imagined the
master suite,
including its
dramatic Moorish
style bathing room,
which features
colorful zellij tile
murals.*

*The loggia serves
as a generously
proportioned
outdoor room.*

be built on four-and-a-half acres they had
purchased in Pasadena on the eastern side of
the Arroyo. The result was a palace in the
Spanish tradition with a hipped tile roof and a
churrigueresque entryway that enlivened the
otherwise subdued appearance of the structure's
exterior. Sadly, the house was literally cut in two
when the property was subdivided in the 1950s,
and the churrigueresque elements were lost.
The large main portion of the house has been
restored to its former grandeur by architect
Erik Evens of KAA Design Group. The former
dining room, the most dramatic room of the
house with its immense walk-in fireplace lined
with Gustavino and old Spanish pictorial tiles,
is now the living room. The once-neglected
grounds have been revived as well by landscape
architect Melinda Taylor, who restored the
reflecting pool and the Persian watercourse
that marries the house to the garden.

22

*The Persian style
water fountain and
a lap pool are among
the garden's many
water features.*

A. I. Root House

Los Feliz, 1924
Carleton Winslow, architect

In 1937, the American Institute of Architects
published Rexford Newcomb's *Spanish Colonial
Architecture in the United States*. Still in print
today, the book is a seminal work on the history
and development of the style and features many
great examples built in and around Los Angeles
in the 1920s and early 30s. The frontispiece to
the book is a photograph of a Spanish fountain
at the home of A. I. Root, designed by Carleton
Winslow in 1924. It remains a quintessential
example of what Newcomb was celebrating.

Built in the hills of Los Feliz, the house
meanders down three stories from the street-
level courtyard into a canyon. From the outside
the house is a mostly pure Spanish with its
troweled stucco and wrought iron details but
there is a nod to the day with slightly Moderne
chevrons capping the buttresses on one towering corner of the house. Inside, an array of
elaborately painted vaults decorate the ceilings
of the various room, most dramatically perhaps
in the parasol shaped design of the dining
room, which is situated in the third-floor
rotunda. Strangely, this wasn't originally a true

indoor-outdoor house. There is a courtyard on the street level, but the house was never integrated into the garden as one would expect. The current owner solved this problem with the help of architect Michael Burch by converting the basement room into a library with French doors that open to the garden. Burch also designed an exterior stairway whose arch projects over the French doors and leads to the second floor.

The owner also unearthed a treasure in the overgrown grounds of the property: an original garden designed by landscape architect Paul Howard, well known "nurseryman" of the 1920s whose public landscapes in the Wilshire district, Hollywood and Pasadena help define the look of the city. With the help of landscape architect Michael Baer, old stone walls emerged, original paths were reestablished, a buried fountain rimmed by Mexican Talavera tiles was restored, and even a box containing the original plans and related clippings was discovered.

Previous pages:
The living room
with beamed
framework ceiling

This page:
Above: The library

Right: A view into
the kitchen. Note
the clever pointed
vault over the door.

The dining room features geometric elements inspired by architectural detailing of the Middle Ages and Renaissance.

Following pages:
Left: Wrought iron workings from an old well in the forecourt

Right: This fountain served as the illustrated frontispiece to Rexford Newcomb's seminal 1937 book Spanish-Colonial Architecture in the United States.

Christiancy Estate

Rancho Santa Fe, 1927
Lilian Rice, architect

Lilian Rice stands among the great women architects of the west alongside Mary Colter, Julia Morgan, and Lutah Maria Riggs. With the firm of Requa and Jackson, she was a pivotal figure in the development of Rancho Santa Fe, which was once the Rancho San Dieguto, later property of the Santa Fe Railroad, and now one of California's most beautiful communities. Rice's many buildings in the area are benchmarks for the simple Spanish style for which the area is known. She defined the look of the community with its little Spanish village town center and the perfect Inn at Rancho Santa Fe, which Rice designed as accommodations for prospective property buyers and is now one of the great boutique hotels.

The George A. C. Christiancy Estate commands the top of a knoll overlooking an idyllic valley reminiscent of the images once found on

Above: Motor court and entry gate leading to the second level courtyard

Right: A view of the house from the garden

The living room is brightened by the light wood beams of the ceiling.

Following pages: The octagonal courtyard serves as an outdoor room and a transition to the interior of the house.

California orange box labels or in real estate booster brochures. The house is accessed atop a flight of stairs that lead to a hexagonal entrance court with an outdoor fireplace. Broken into levels that follow the slope downward, the two-and-a-half-story home complements the topography more than dictating to it. On the lushly landscaped grounds, there are numerous fountains, including an Adamson peacock fountain next to the pool and guest house, and an exceptional use of tile. Over the years, Rice made changes to the house, one of which was the addition of bay windows to afford the best views of the valley below.

Above: A view past the pool to the rolling hills of Rancho Santa Fe

Right: The peacock fountain by the pool was inspired by the one at the Adamson House in Malibu (p. 304).

Following pages: Water spills from all points of this quatrefoil fountain. Also note the blending of brick and tile in the paving.

44

Left: Entry foyer, facing the richly carved front door

Right: The front facade of the timeless house

Prindle House

Pasadena, 1926
George Washington Smith, architect

George Washington Smith settled in the Santa Barbara suburb of Montecito around 1917. A painter first, he received some architectural training at Harvard, which he put to use in building himself a house and studio inspired by the Andalusian farmhouses he admired while living in Europe. The choice seemed appropriate given the similar Mediterranean climates, and it would fare better in wildfires than the neighboring wooden-shingled Queen Annes and Victorians. The architecture also seemed appropriate in its kinship to the Spanish missions so closely associated with the region. The neighbors took notice: by the time of his death in 1930, Smith's Spanish Colonial style had redefined the architectural look of Southern California and given the area such landmarks as Casa del Herrero and the Lobero Theater in Santa Barbara.

The Prindle House is still in the family it was designed for and is one of only a few Smith did

in Pasadena. The architect designed the house with the close involvement of the clients, traveling with them to Italy, Spain, and Morocco in search of authentic elements to incorporate into the house. They returned with antique tile, light fixtures, iron, furniture, and Mudéjar doors that were all custom-fitted into the house. The result is a dramatic Spanish Colonial Revival–style house built around a courtyard. Beyond an Islamic star-shaped fountain, antique mosque doors open from the courtyard into a garden almost certainly inspired by those at Granada. The antique Spanish and Italian furniture, decorative art, tapestries, and paintings in the public rooms are all as they were when the house was decorated.

Above: From the entry hall, a glimpse of the living room's large hooded fireplace

Right: A view into the dining room, virtually unchanged for almost 85 years

Left: The courtyard and gardens are clearly inspired by those at the Alhambra in Spain.

Right: A deep niche for a tiled wash basin

Following pages: The eight-pointed star is the central form from which the Moroccan zillij patterns evolve. As with this fountain, it also serves as an apropos nucleus to a courtyard garden.

Steedman Estate

Casa del Herrero, Montecito, 1925
George Washington Smith, architect

Casa del Herrero, the house George Fox Steedman, a St. Louis industrialist, and his wife, Carrie, built in Santa Barbara on 11 acres in 1925 survives today as one of the finest American country homes on the west coast. While certainly a crowning achievement for architect George Washington Smith—architectural historian David Gebhard referred to it as one of the very finest of Smith's Andalusian villas—the estate is the result of the work of a team of highly talented people, Steedman included. He was the ironworker that gave the house its name (House of the Blacksmith), and he worked closely with Smith, landscape architects Ralph K. Stevens, Francis T. Underhill, and Lockwood de Forest Jr., and architect Lutah Maria Riggs, who designed the house's stunning octagonal library. Steedman's attention to detail is evident everywhere one looks, from his own iron details and abundant Tunisian tile to sunken fountains and fine woodwork. Thank-

Above: A view toward the walled western garden

Right: The north facade

Previous pages:
The living room with
the Steedmans'
furnishings and
portraits

Left: The entry hall

Right: Dining room
and corner fireplace
with a glazed pointed
hood

fully, as has often been the case with properties of this scale, none of the 11 acres were ever sub-divided.

With its numerous patios, courtyards, and now mature gardens, the casa remains in the family, who created the nonprofit Casa del Her-rero Foundation with the goal of restoring and preserving the house and grounds. In addition to this, Casa del Herrero is listed on the National Register of Historic Places and was made a National Historic Landmark in 2009.

Left: The loggia

Below left: A tile bench in the garden

Right: Spanish courtyard garden

Following pages: The Pepper Tree garden with a fountain designed by Arthur Byne

Wilson House

Robledal, Hope Ranch, Santa Barbara, 1920
George Washington Smith, architect

Known as Robledal after the oak grove surrounding it, this sprawling George Washington Smith courtyard estate was designed for Milton Wilson, one of the original developers of Hope Ranch, an equestrian community overlooking the Pacific Ocean next to Santa Barbara. It is a great example of how a large house can be sensitively integrated with its natural surroundings. Though the main house suffered the indignity of losing its second-floor bedrooms, the now extended 14,000-square foot single-story home's lower profile melds well with its neighboring trees and gardens. Many signature Smith details remain, including thick carved mahogany doors, iron gates, sconces and

Above: Through the entry gate at Robledal

Right: View from motor court toward the guest quarters

Following pages: The living room

*Previous pages:
A variety of floor,
beam, and door
patterns seen along
the hall*

*Right:Thanks to the
garden's abundant
crawlers the
architecture
disappears into the
landscape.*

chandeliers, and beautiful tiled floors. The
sunken entry hall, dining room, and living room
are expansive and retain their ornate ceilings
and woodwork.

The walled entry courtyard is accessed
through a gate covered by a clay tile roof. The
front door is graced by a similar tiled hood.
Additional patios open to the gardens at various
points and an enclosed loggia offers a quiet
transition from the house to the surrounding
gardens and fountains.

72

Sherwood House

La Jolla, 1928
George Washington Smith, architect

George Washington Smith's association with Santa Barbara and Montecito is well known, but he did work of equal quality 180 miles south in the beautiful Orange County community of La Jolla. Built for California artist Franklin P. Sherwood, this house, situated on a magnificent rocky point right on the Pacific Ocean, stands in elegant defiance of the elements. Its bold facade features round piercings, decorative wrought iron window screens, and a bracketed wall lantern featuring a seabird clutching a lamp. A dramatic carved wooden *mashrabiyah*, an exterior wall screen in the Islamic tradition, filters air and light into a second-floor suite. Two pointed stucco and clay tile chimney stacks grace the shallow pitched roof.

Neither the house nor garden appears to have been changed, thankfully. A unique sculptural staircase with a thick banister bends from

Above: The house sits perched on a knoll overlooking the Pacific Ocean.

Right: A view from the beach looking toward the house

the foyer to a projecting bay on the second floor creating a dynamic geometric blend in white stucco. Incorporated antique elements include a wooden framed Moorish niche similar to one found at Casa del Herrero, as well as Renaissance-era panels. Roses and bougainvillea thrive in the rear courtyard garden, which is shielded from the unforgiving ocean wind by the house and surrounding walls. Central to the garden courtyard plan are four Tunisian tiled benches surrounding a fountain, which is fed via a narrow rivulet leading from a similarly tiled wall fountain.

Right: The living room

Following pages: Left: A view of the Pacific Ocean

Right: The dining room

The plastered
banister with
its classical and
modernistic
sculptural features

Following pages:
Four simple tile
benches surround
a sunken fountain
in the garden.

Left: *A tiled passageway leading to the front door*

Right: *Steps leading to the entry framed by native plantings*

Ford House

Ojai, 1929
Paul Williams, architect

William Ford, a cousin of Henry Ford and business partner of Edward Drummond Libbey, followed Libbey out west to settle in the rural California town of Ojai in 1929. Together they owned the Libbey-Ford Glass Company, which made safety glass windshields for the Model A as well as Coca-Cola bottles. Libbey was instrumental in the development of the community, hiring such luminaries as Wallace Neff and Richard Requa to build everything from the town's clubhouse to its major civic structures. Ojai, a stunningly beautiful region of gently rolling hills dotted with oak trees north of Santa Barbara, was well on its way to establishing itself as a bastion of great Revival architecture.

84

To design his Spanish-style courtyard house, Ford selected architect Paul Williams, whom he may have met through automobile manufacturer Errett L. Cord for whom Williams had designed an extraordinary Southern Colonial mansion in Beverly Hills. Set on a fine knoll overlooking the Ojai Mountains, famous for their pink sunsets, Ford's house, like Cord's, was designed without budget limitations but with a more thoughtful restraint than the earlier project. Williams ran with the opportunity to showcase his talents working in the Spanish Revival style for which he was not known. Built to last, the large two-story house was constructed on skyscraper steel I-beams somehow transported to the site. He arranged the house around a large courtyard with a long rivulet leading to the central fountain. The main entrance leads to a large enclosed loggia on the first floor. The second floor boasts a pair of large open-air patios overlooking a Williams-designed pool and the bucolic meadows and mountains beyond. The current owners have recently completed a four-year historic restoration, returning the estate known as La Collina Ranch to its original condition and honoring the genius of this rare Paul Williams hacienda.

Previous pages:
The bedroom suite

Left: Looking down
into the central
courtyard garden

Right: Steps from
the second-story
inner balcony
leading down to the
garden

Above: A cozy patio

Right: The dry garden is punctuated by citrus trees. The fountain provides an oasis in the center.

Following pages: Tile detail with fish motif

Pages 98-99: Rear facade with original Williams-designed pool

Gould House

Montecito, 1918
Reginald Johnson, architect

Above: Approaching the entry porch

Right: From the driveway one sees the home enveloped by oaks.

Following pages: Plain bold columns support the roof over the large patio.

George Jay Gould, son of robber baron Jay Gould, and heir to his railroad fortune, settled with his wife Lillian in Santa Barbara in 1917. They purchased eight acres of land and commissioned venerable architect Reginald Johnson to build their residence. Johnson's reputation as

100

Previous pages:
Left: A decorative
iron flourish on the
front door screen

Right: View from
the foyer into the
living room

These pages:
The living room

Following pages:
Mature vines on
a trellis create a
natural loggia,
which is surrounded
by eucalyptus trees.

the preeminent architect of the region at the time was well founded. His landmark Biltmore Hotel set the precedent for many of the area's great estates and he had recently completed Miraflores, the Montecito estate for which he later won the AIA gold medal—something of a coup for a Los Angeles architect at the time.

For the Goulds, Johnson designed a generous California *hacienda* with signature low-pitched shingled roofs around a gated courtyard. The five-bedroom home has many old-world details: heavy sculpted beams, wooden storm shutters, and iron oak-leaf wall sconces add timeless character to this great old home. Facing west, a pergola envelops a seating area with views of the ocean framed in vines and grand old trees. A deep portico shelters the entrances from the main courtyard and once provided an outdoor room sufficient for both horse and rider for the former equestrian estate.

Left: *An outdoor fireplace and brick oven*

Right: *A covered patio wraps around the courtyard allowing for outdoor dining.*

Collins House

Los Feliz, 1933
Norstrom & Anderson, architects

The firm of Milton L. Anderson and Alvin E. Norstrom are remembered primarily for their retail projects in and around Los Angeles in the 1930s and 40s, especially their Late Moderne buildings around the old Third Street Promenade in Santa Monica. Their earliest work, however, was a row of Spanish Colonial Revival–style storefronts on Second Street in downtown Los Angeles. Not long after completing these, they also finished this house in Los Feliz.

Built for the managing editor of the *Los Angeles Evening Herald* Edwin R. Collins and his wife, Margaret, in the historic enclave of Los Feliz, this house is one of many significant

Spanish Colonials in the area. Entered through a large radial arch, the house has a number of distinguishing characteristics, including a Mission-style bell tower off of one corner, and, wrapping around another corner, a large clay-tile covered balcony projecting over a hillside garden. Brick columns support a covered patio that straddles the main courtyard. Over the years, architect Michael Burch has modified much of the property, including reworking the courtyard hardscaping around a grand old oak tree, adding a tile fountain, and building a new guest house to match the main residence.

The sunny living room has a spare Mission quality.

Top: An impressive balcony juts off the side of the hill.

Right: The pool is set amongst succulents and cacti.

Above: The front door recessed in a deep arch

Following pages: The large tiled fountain is home to a lily pond.

Barker House

La Canada Flintridge, 1922
Myron Hunt, architect

During his 50-year architectural career, Myron Hunt left his influential mark all over the Los Angeles region. His most familiar landmark may be the Rose Bowl in Pasadena, but, with partners H. C. Chambers and Elmer Grey, he also did important work on the campuses of Occidental and Pomona colleges, along with a number of lofty residential commissions, most notably the San Marino home of Henry Edwards Huntington.

This hacienda-style house, named La Casa Bonita, was built for Earle Barker, son of O. T. Barker, who founded Southern California's oldest furniture chain, Barker Brothers, in 1880, when the population of Los Angeles was a mere 11,000. The shallow roof projects beyond the walls of the main wing in both directions, creating long covered patios on both sides of the

Above: Running the length of the house, the patio roof is supported by helical columns.

Right: The house is surrounded by lush grass and iceberg roses.

A glimpse of the night sky painted on the hall ceiling

Highly detailed, hand-painted follies and emblemata decorate ceilings and doors throughout the house.

Right: A view into the living room.

Left: A stylized coat of arms depicting a double-headed eagle

Right: The living room's textured walls and antique mantle

Following pages: Left: Decorative painting and stained glass adorn the hallway.

Right: The eclectic array of design elements found throughout the house climax with the chinoiserie bedroom.

Pages 126–27: Left: A handsome bird amongst grapevines in iron

Right: Original to the home, bells hang from iron staffs as a greeting in the entry court.

house. The rear private side, with its shuttered windows and grape-themed iron screens, faces a grassy brick-paved courtyard and fountain. The house retains its original decorative painting, including highly elaborate grotesque doors and ceilings as well as its amazing—and totally incongruous—Chinoiserie room. Adding to the theatrics, the vaulted hall ceiling features a painting of the night sky.

Longan Estate

El Castillo del Lago, Hollywoodland, 1926
John DeLario, architect

Hollywoodland is the locale that set the standard for the way of life described by the phrase, "living in the Hollywood Hills." The way into the area was bulldozed and paved by Albert Beach, whose namesake road, Beachwood Drive, is still the main path into those hills. The neighborhood got its name from the large sign on a hillside overlooking the community, built at the suggestion of *Los Angeles Times* publisher Harry Chandler. For a while, the sign was even lit, but it proved flimsy and eventually lost the last four letters down the hillside, leaving the famous "Hollywood" sign as we know it today.

The towering approach of El Castillo del Lago

(text continues on p. 137)

Far left: A grand stenciled balcony looms over the foyer.

Left: The living room, off of a long stretch of arches, has a tall hooded corner fireplace and great painted beams.

Right: A hand-wrought iron mythical beast caps a banister.

Following pages: Left: The dining room

Top right: The library

Bottom right: Breakfast room

*Left: Looking down
the tower's
staggering five-
story spiral staircase*

*Below: A view from
a balcony of the
Hollywood reservoir,
and, in the distance,
the Pacific Ocean*

135

*Left: Vines
meander up the
Castillio's many
stair walls.*

*Right: A view of
the inner courtyard
and main tower*

*Following paes:
Looking up the hill
toward the
neighbors. Parts of
old Hollywoodland
are reminiscent of
Mediterranean hill
towns.*

(text continued from page 128)

Architect John DeLario built the first building in Beachwood Canyon, a sales and promotional office, still standing, for developer S. H. Woodruff. He went on to build a number of the area's commercial structures and landmark houses. The most famous of these is the one built for oil explorer Patrick Longan. With its 20,000 square feet, nine levels, endless staircases, and $250,000 price tag, El Castillo del Lago was an instant landmark. Sadly, Longan's wife died upon its completion, and Longan chose to move on. After many years of neglect and an unsympathetic tongue-in-cheek remodel, a caring owner has now lovingly restored the *castillo*, which can be seen towering above the Hollywood reservoir from all across town.

Burnham House

Capo di Monte, Hollywoodland, 1927
Joseph J. Blick, architect

To fully grasp the geographic overview of Los Angeles and its environs, one needs to view the city from a jetliner or from the perch selected by former military scout and oilman Frederick Burnham for his home in 1927. The house, on its dramatic two-acre site just above El Castillo del Lago, is another Hollywoodland classic.

Christened Capo di Monte, it was designed by architect Joseph J. Blick, who, in the early 1900s, built a number of homes in the Craftsman style popularized by Charles and Henry Greene in the Pasadena area. Though this house is clearly a Spanish Revival design, there seems to be an Arts and Crafts influence in the well-maintained and original interiors, which feature wood floors and exposed beams of a very light hue and lack the usual stenciling and adornment. The overall simplicity of the house, with its functional rooms and lack of ornament, also exhibits Modern leanings evident in the arched cast-concrete entryway. Blick paid care-

Above: A path at the top of the hill leads around the side of the house to the entrance.

Right: The deep-set, cast-concrete doorway adds a modern touch to the otherwise traditional facade.

ful attention to each room's orientation, making the most of the dramatic vistas: from the various windows one has striking views of downtown to the east, the San Fernando Valley and the Simi Hills to the north, the port of Long Beach to the south, and the beaches of Santa Monica to the far west.

Previous pages: Left: An antique vargueno once owned by Cecil B. DeMille

Right: The house is uncharacteristically bright and airy for the style, thanks to well placed windows and the light stain of the woodwork.

Above: Though a period revival house, the high white walls and somewhat open floor plan are at home with Eames furniture and abstract paintings, including this one by Frederick Sauls.

Right: In the living room, a suite of Barcelona furniture designed by Mies van der Rohe. A Frederic Matys Thursz painting hangs next to the fireplace with surround of Ernest Batchelder tile.

144

Above: A quintessential California plein-air scene viewed through the windows of the breakfast nook, accompanied by a second scene painted by Pasadena artist Louis Hovey Sharp.

Right: From the balcony, a view over the reservoir to greater Los Angeles below

146

Chimorro House

Beverly Hills, 1926
Roy Sheldon Price, architect

Prohibition inadvertently created a niche in the world of design with many a home built between 1919 and 1933 containing a speakeasy. Sometimes, they were elaborate rooms hidden behind faux panels; sometimes, they were modest nooks hidden beyond a closet; and, in a few cases, the entire house was designed to accommodate such wants. Hidden behind imposing wooden gates, walled and secure, the Chimorro residence is a true prohibition house.

Designed by Roy Sheldon Price, architect of the 1929 Los Angeles landmark built for Charlie Chaplin that now houses the Campanile restaurant and the sadly demolished Días Dorado compound for Thomas Ince, this

Above: The house is situated sideways on its lot.

Right: An arching staircase leads up to a long balcony, later added by architect Brian Tichenor.

148

two-story house, with its long balcony and rounded white plaster walls, has magnificent presence. The large public rooms were clearly designed for contemporary entertaining, including the safeguard of windows with sight lines that would provide ample warning of approaching police. The interiors of the thick and hollow walls could be accessed through a number of hidden doors where upwards of 70 people could hide if necessary. Its primary function aside, this generously proportioned Spanish house next to the Beverly Hills Hotel is a gem and has been beautifully restored by the architectural firm of Tichenor & Thorp. An architect as well as a landscape architect, Brian Tichenor also designed the gardens with their Islamic-inspired water channels that lead to small burbling fountains.

Previous pages; The main hall steps lead from the dining room through thick passageways to the living room, decorated by Annie Kelly.

These pages: Cleverly shaded by a canopy, this private courtyard has its own fireplace and a coat of arms, like the one by the front door, pierced in the wall.

Among the garden's water features, added by architect Brian Tichenor, are Moroccan-inspired spillways and fountains. Water dances from a separate fountain in the middle of the swimming pool.

Left: Through a vine covered arch, the long arcade leading to the front door

Right: The home's rambling tiled roofs and towers are said to have been inspired by villages near Seville, Spain.

Sills-Kenyon House

Brentwood, 1927
Architect unknown

M ilton Sills left his native Chicago and academic life as a psychology and philosophy professor at the University of Chicago to pursue stage acting in 1905. He found success, and, in 1914, his career segued into the new medium of motion pictures. He eventually worked his way up to leading man, and, in 1924, starred opposite Colleen Moore in the MGM blockbuster *The Sea Hawk*.

The year 1927 was one to celebrate for this man of letters who landed in Hollywood: he and his wife, silent film actress Doris Kenyon, had a son whom they named Kenyon Clarence Sills; he joined Douglas Fairbanks, Harold Lloyd, Mary Pickford, and 32 others to form

Left: A beautiful
staircase with
impressive iron
banister rises
under a vaulted
ceiling, decorated
with a mural
depicting stories of
architectural and
art history.

Right: Mother
Mary presides over
the centuries-old,
nail-studded front
doors, locked the
old fashioned way.

Following pages:
Left: Stairs in the
back courtyard lead
up to a guest
apartment.

Right: A view
through a patio
wall to the garden
beyond.

Left: One of many unique iron window grills on the property

Right: A tiled bench built against the house off of the garden

the Academy of Motion Picture Arts and Sciences; and, lastly, he saw the completion of his dream house in Brentwood.

Affectionately dubbed *El Sueño del Halcon del Mar* (The Sea Hawk's Dream), the house was modeled after the Andalusian homes the Sills had seen while traveling in Spain, while also giving a nod to the nautical theme of his films. Through a leafy arch, a long corridor leads to the ancient nail-studded front door. The house incorporates Italian and Spanish antiques, including Renaissance-era iron window grills, glazed Della Robbia pottery, hand-carved wooden columns as well as tiles with Spanish galleon motifs, mooring poles, and old chain. Plaques from an old Spanish cathedral are recessed into thick stucco walls and some 150 corbels from a dismantled castle near Seville accent beams throughout the house. The vaulted ceiling above the entryway is painted with a mural depicting the arts. One of the panels revealed the identity of the man who designed the house, Stephen Goosson. Goosson was an Academy Award winning art director who did the designs for *The Sea Hawk*, and the film's influence on the house is evident.

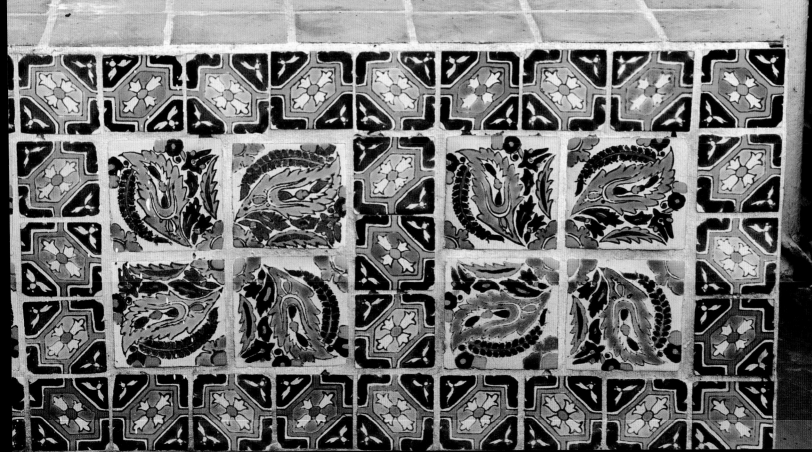

McNeil House

Beverly Hills, 1926
Wallace Neff, architect

This 1926 house in the flats of Beverly Hills, with its oval entryway, circular staircase, and checkered floor, is a signature Wallace Neff. Neff, a student of American Gothic Revival–style architect Ralph Adams Cram, was the quintessential architect of the era. Though he designed major commissions in a variety of period revival styles, his mastery of the Spanish Mediterranean style will likely be his legacy. The McNeil house escaped the fate of many others by being left virtually untouched for 70 years, preserving Neff's vision unfettered by unwise renovation. Many of the house's original elements survive, including pocket doors that open from the living room out to the garden, an intricate iron banister in the entryway, and the fireplace andirons. But the benign neglect also demonstrated what the accumulation of 70 years of fireplace smoke can do to a fine painted wooden ceiling.

Above: The enclosed balcony overlooks a private garden.

Right: Wrought iron balconies perch over the large vaulted entryway.

164

Previous pages:
Left: Mosaic tile
seems to spill from
this fountain across
the floor of the
sunroom.

Right: The large
arched vaults in
this room echo those
of the house entry.

These pages:
Left: A dreamy
astrological-themed
mural on the
ceiling over the
stairway

Right: The grand
stairway winds up
to the second floor.

The living room

*Following pages:
A detail of one of
the finely painted
beams, which was
restored after
suffering smoke
damage.*

The current owners have done an extensive
restoration: the painted ceiling in the living
room was cleaned, oiled, and hand waxed; the
paneling and bookcases in the library, all original, were stripped, sanded, and re-stained; and
the original wooden front door was replaced by
a custom wrought iron design that matches the
staircase banister. The floors did not have the
typical tiled wainscoting, so the owners added
the border using new tiles from Morocco.

The house and grounds were enlarged with
the addition of the adjacent southern lot where
the existing house was torn down to make room
for expanded gardens, an outdoor dining area,
and a smaller guest house, a seemingly counter-
intuitive move in a city becoming more known
for new McMansions built to the edges of their
property lines. Through increased open space,
the owners have been able to create their own
dreamy arcadia.

Above: The dining room

Right: The updated kitchen ceiling is a whimsical nod to the tile arts.

Following pages: Gravel surrounds a koi pond in the garden.

The towering front facade

Hanson House

La Canada Flintridge, 1919
Henry Harwood Hewitt, architect

Built for Illinois transplants Mr. and Mrs. George Hanson between 1919 and 1922, this 14-room, Moorish-influenced, Spanish Revival–style castle boasts five levels, a two-story coffered barrel foyer, and winding staircases. The rambling levels viewed from the foyer up and through the house bring to mind the designs of M. C. Escher. It was designed by architect Henry Harwood Hewitt, a graduate of Massachusetts Institute of Technology and later the École des Beaux-Arts in Paris. The overall result of his design is that of a folly and demonstrates the lengths some obliging architects went when a deep-pocketed client dreamed big. Hewitt did not worry about purity here: with elements such as faux Roman goddesses serving as columns and arabesques murals reminiscent of those at Pompeii covering the hulking vaulted ceiling in the living room, the house travels in a few

*Below: Looking
through a Juliette
window, with its
Ernest Batchelder-
designed tile
surround and small
fountain, toward the
dining room*

*Right: The living
room with grand
arched ceiling*

different directions. If anything, this collision
of European antiquity in the Mediterranean
reminds us of our often muddled sense of
history. In the grand scheme of things, cherry-
picking elements from architectural history is
nothing new, and the resulting melting pot is
what can give birth to new traditions.

Previous pages:
Left: In a ceiling detail, Pan surveys the rooms below.

Right: The multi-story entry foyer

Above: A potted garden on the back patio

Right: Whimsical columns supporting the loggia demonstrate that the family had a sense of humor about their home.

Following pages: A view of the back of the house seen from the pool

Hacienda Mojica

Santa Monica Canyon, 1929
Merrill W. Baird, architect

Entering the gardens of Hacienda Mojica is like being transported to another place and time. The property sits on what was once part of the Rancho Boca de Santa Monica, a Mexican land grant given to Francisco Marquez and Ysidro Reyes in 1839. Through the tile-hooded gate with an inscribed dedication to the Virgin of Guadalupe, the *entrada* leads to a courtyard, gardens, and house just as one would find in the Mexican countryside. The *hacienda* was built by the opera singer José Mojica for his mother, who lost her estate in Mexico during the secularization. This was a way for him to give her back her home.

While Merrill W. Baird is credited as the architect, it has long been believed to be the work of John Byers and does bear many of the hallmarks of his work. A self-taught architect, Byers was an early proponent of the Hispanic

Above: Old gates in the garden

Right: Mature hydrangeas bloom in the forecourt of Hacienda Mojica.

Following pages: Left: The hacienda's private chapel

Right: The foyer and its unique chandelier

building tradition, including adobe construction methods. He was highly regarded as a designer of many fine Spanish-style houses on the west side of Los Angeles. His allied studio employed a team of talented craftsmen, many from Mexico, who, in turn, built many more structures, often uncredited. Today, there remain many noted "possible" John Byers houses.

Baird was a draftsman in Byers office and may have inherited this project. The house was later owned by actress Anita Loos of *Gentlemen Prefer Blondes* fame, who, for nearly three decades preserved the house and promoted its connection to California's Spanish and Mexican heritage. Today, the *hacienda* serves as La Señora Research Institute, a nonprofit dedicated to documenting the history of the rancho era of early California, particularly as it relates to Rancho Boca de Santa Monica, and helps to protect its small Marquez cemetery, which dates to the 1840s and is protected behind an adobe wall put there by John Byers.

*Previous pages:
Left: An old
Moorish door*

*Right: Patio with
recessed panel
depicting the Virgin
of Guadalupe*

*These pages:
Above: The chapel
from the garden*

*Right: Doors
leading to the
courtyard garden,
which features
everything from
climbing roses to
citrus trees and tall
artichokes*

*Above: A tile map
of early California
depicting its
Spanish roots and
the missions
established in
Nueva España*

*Right: Tall
eucalyptus trees and
birds-of-paradise
sprout in the court-
yard by the pool.*

196

Left: Front door
with magnificent
tile surround

Right: The essential
elements of a
Spanish house—red
tile, white stucco,
and wrought
iron—mange to
peak through the
trees and
hydrangeas from
the approach.

Long House

Brentwood, 1927
Architect unknown

Built for the family of real estate broker Lewis E. Long in a Brentwood neighborhood closely associated with Byers, this house, although uncredited, exhibits many of the fine characteristics found in larger projects attributed to Byers. In the later 1930s, it became home to Dutch Consul Adrian Hartog, later Dean Emeritus of the Los Angeles Consular Corps. With high beamed ceilings, tiled and hardwood floors, and iron sconces and rails, the house has all the elements one would hope for in a well-done Spanish Revival home. A beautifully tiled recessed entryway frames the nail-studded front door through which one is greeted by piles of books and old Hollywood film posters. Up tile-faced steps, a series of arches lead to the various rooms. Windows look through wooden spin-

dled screens out to lush landscaping. The court area is generously planted with both roses and tropical plants, and, with its pool, is a real oasis.

The owner's collection of modern and contemporary furnishings blends well with the historic character of the house, with its dark floors, beams, and voluminous rooms.

Above: A bit of the French Riviera appears in the breakfast room.

Right: A variety of interesting furniture is found in the house, including this great Thonet rocker in the living room.

Below: Red walls and a Fornasetti chandelier add drama to the dining room.

Right: An image of Charlie Chaplin peaks out through an arch on the landing, serving as a reminder of the fondness Hollywood has always had for evocative Spanish Revival houses.

Following pages: Left: A small courtyard potted garden

Right: A perfect outdoor dining room

Pages 206–07: The mature garden hugs a pool at the back of the house.

202

Rosson House

Brentwood, 1923
John Byers, architect

Built in 1923, John Byers designed this house for Harold Rosson, famed cinematographer best known for his award winning work on *The Wizard of Oz*, but also remembered for his brief marriage to actress Jean Harlow. The white brick facade and two-tiered, red clay-tiled roof are anchored by a wide two-door entry capped by a one-and-a-half-story tower with a crossed oculus window. Around it, the grounds have matured and the house has grown.

Working from Byers' original plan, noted architect Marc Appleton has greatly expanded the house, enveloped by lush landscaping by some 7,500 square feet. The house has the feel of an easy California Spanish Mediterranean designed for outdoor dining and entertaining. The interior is light-filled thanks to well placed

Above: The motor court garden

Right: The front doors are flanked by a pair of Moroccan-style lanterns and adorned with devotional paintings.

208

Below: The dining room

Right: The tastefully updated kitchen

French doors that also offer direct views into the garden. Despite its old world qualities, the house is functional and has been adapted well to contemporary needs both indoors and out. Hardscaping, made up of broken concrete with pebble mosaics incorporated into the grout surrounds the house, forming paths that lead through gardens designed by landscape architect April Palmer.

210

Below: A courtyard perfect for lounging

Right: Outdoor dining fireside, with Mexican equipale chairs around an old table

Wanberg House

Hacienda Heights, 1931
Frank O. Eager, architect

The nearly 30-acre ranch outside of Los Angeles, owned by philanthropist George E. Wanberg, was affectionately known as *Rancho el Valle Feliz*, Ranch of the Happy Valley. Between 1912 and 1928 the property was mainly used for orange groves, a common sight across Southern California at this time. Dr. Wanberg commissioned architect Frank O. Eager to build a country house for him and his wife, Maye, on the grounds, which was completed in 1931. Working in the newly popularized Spanish Colonial Revival style, Eager added touches of whimsy to this house that make it unique: a stone grotto protects the entryway; cylinders topped with colorful pottery resembling ice cream cones climb a staircase in the garden; and a thick rope threaded through an elaborate iron template

Above: Looking across handmade red clay tiles toward a unique chimney

Right: A stone grotto before the entryway

Previous pages:
Left: An iron rail turns the corner at the top of the stairs.

Right: An iron-supported rope banister steps down the staircase

Below: A great pairing of doors and decorative tile

Right: Period furnishings and antiques in the living room

serves as a baluster leading up the main staircase in the foyer. Throughout the house, one finds a mix of Claycraft and Calco tile, along with a variety of antiques. The stucco is rough, and the clay roofing tiles show the striations of workers' fingers, giving the impression of a house built by hand.

Following pages: Detail of rough-hewn ceiling beam and corbel

218

Previous pages:
The dining room.
Note the recessed
cabinetry.

Above: Pottery on
a tiled windowsill

Right: The lovely
period kitchen,
looking into the
breakfast room

Following pages:
Playful garden
ornaments dance up
a back wall.

Steinbeck House

Echo Park, 1930
Architect unknown

This good house in the old Los Angeles neighborhood of Echo Park, near Dodger Stadium
and what was once Chavez Ravine, was built for
Henry Steinbeck, cousin of *The Grapes of Wrath*
author John Steinbeck, in 1930 as part of a
planned development of small Spanish Revival
houses. As a result of the Great Depression, the
development was halted, and the building
records have disappeared. Only this and one
other house in the plan were completed. Spanish-style bungalows were built all over Southern
California at the time, but this hillside example
is not typical and it has really been brought to
life with numerous decorative embellishments
and additions by its enthusiastic current owners.

With the exception of the original stenciled
beams, all the decorative painting in the house
was done by Michael Uhlenkott, who also
designed the new decorative tile in the house,

*Above: View of the
rear facade from the
pool area*

*Right: From the
street, the
quintessential
Spanish bungalow
appears to be only a
single-story house.*

228

including a mural by the front door, the stair risers in the living room, the downstairs bathroom, and other small murals on exterior walls. He also added tile to the pool and designed the wall fountain on the lower deck. All of the decorative tiles were made by Diana Mauser of Native Tile in Torrance, California. Alan Smart created the stained glass windows for the living room and also collaborated with Michael Uhlenkott on other elements such as the balconies, plantings, and hardscaping.

Above: The kitchen

*Right: The guest
bath with old
Hollywood western
ephemera*

*Above: Tile detail
from the garden*

*Right: The lower
patio with tile
topped tables and
iron furniture*

Cotton Estate

Casa Pacifica, San Clemente, 1926
Carl Lindbom, architect

Built during the heyday of San Clemente, a scenic seaside development founded by Ole Hanson, who also designed the nearby landmark estate Casa Romantica, this house is steeped in American political history. The early owner, influential Democratic Party backer Hamilton H. Cotton, held fundraisers at the house and hosted President Franklin D. Roosevelt for late-night poker games in the estate's round gazebo overlooking the ocean. The house changed hands, and parties, in 1969 when newly elected President Richard Nixon purchased it as his presidential retreat. Architect Carl Lindbom had called the house *Casa Pacifica* (House of Peace), and this continued to seem fitting given that it is where Nixon and Leonid Brezhnev met to sign the second phase of the Strategic Arms Limitation Treaty.

Above: Urns decorate a section of the garden path.

Right: Looking through the main entry hall leading into the central courtyard

Looking from the library into the dining room

Inspired by a Spanish country house in San Sebastian and situated on an awe-inspiring knoll overlooking famed surf spot Trestles, the grounds of the walled compound are accented with Monterey cypress, pines, palms, and other great trees. One particular magnolia was purportedly grown from a cutting made by First Lady Pat Nixon from one at the White House planted by the wife of President Andrew Jackson. Richly detailed tiled wainscoting and tile-bordered arches accent the house. The pebbled central courtyard garden is centered on an elaborate mosaic-tile fountain accented by whimsical fired-clay frogs.

Left: French doors let light and air into the dining room.

Right: Looking past the foyer through an arched hallway

Left: A tasting table in the wine cellar

Right: A recessed oculus window lets some natural light into the cellar.

Above: Loggia off the courtyard garden. Note the tiled floor.

Right: The great central courtyard with its large outdoor fireplace and stepped fountain with signature frogs

Kelly House

La Canada Flintridge, 1925
Arthur Kelly, architect

With its wide-sloping red clay tile roof and three-quarter rotunda entrance, the house architect Arthur Kelly built for himself in the hills of Alta Canada proved a worthy calling card for larger commissions to come, including Western star William S. Hart's Horseshoe Ranch and the now infamous Playboy Mansion. The house was used in brochures to promote the surrounding development today known as La Canada Flintridge. Kelly got his start in the offices of the well-established and prolific Southern California architect, Elmer Grey.

Designed with architectural partner Joseph Estep, the house features an exterior stuccoed "Jazz" finish and interior stenciled beams. Architects Diane Wilk and Michael Burch did a major addition to the house, practically douling its size, while seamlessly blending old with new architcture. They also designed the garden on the sloping hillside and the pool, from where, on a clear day, one can glimpse downtown Los Angeles through the trees.

The entry tower, once two separate floors, was opened up by architects Michael Burch and Diane Wilk to create a dramatic two-story entry.

246

The living room

Following pages:
Left: A small tiled
nook and washbasin

Right: Architects
Diane Wilk and
Michael Burke
designed the
curving stairwell
that leads to the
lower portion of the
house, utilizing bold
tile wainscoting and
a turned iron
guardrail and
banister.

Above: View of rear terrace. On a clear day, Los Angeles peaks through the trees.

Right: Looking up toward the rear facade from a dining area in the garden

Earl Estate

La Canada Flintridge, 1926
Everett Babcock, architect

In his sadly short career, architect Everett Babcock made a name for himself in Southern California with notable houses and commercial structures such as the Singer Building in old town Pasadena. Originally from New York, Babcock practiced in the state of Washington before moving to Pasadena with his wife around 1923. His first job was in Wallace Neff's office where he likely refined his talent for designing in the Spanish Colonial Revival style.

After establishing his own practice, one of his first solo commissions was for William Jarvis Earl, son of the founder of the new Alta Canada tract, Edwin T. Earl. As with Arthur Kelly's house, this also served as a model for the type of home being promoted in this burgeoning, prestigious neighborhood. With its undulating plaster, hipped and gabled clay tile roof, and deep-set windows and doors, the Earl house has many of the elements of a quintessential Spanish Californian. But Babcock also added some

A picture of paradise, among lush plantings brightened by blooming clivia.

254

unique touches of his own. In a clever solution to the challenge of adapting to a sloped lot, an arched colonnade steps down alongside the garden. As well, detailed tooling of the projecting timber beams oer the front door add drama to the facade.

Over the years the once large parcel of land the house sat on was subdivided, ultimately requiring a reorientation of the approach, accomplished by architects Michael Burch and Diane Wilk. A new driveway was established along with reworked walkways and new courtyards. Burch added tile, colored bottle glass, and a new fountain that blend well with the existing design.

Above: A cozy fireplace flanked by recessed bookcases in the living room fosters a sense of intimacy and warmth.

Right: Arches and their shadows add depth and dimension throughout the house.

Following pages: Left: An iron torchère

Middle: Bottle-bottom glass enlivens a round window.

Right: Another view of the arched hallway approaching the entrance.

Left: Entry court

Bottom left:
A graceful,
columned archway
works its way down
the sloped garden.

Right: Architect
Michael Burch
added the tiled
fountain and
hardscape.

Gosser House

Hancock Park, 1928
Milton Black, architect

This colorful example designed by Milton Black stands in contrast to the typical white stucco finish one is used to seeing. The peach patina is an intended match to the architect's original hue. In windows, over doors, and running under banisters, hundreds of intricately tooled and hand-painted spindles accent the house, keeping a painter employed year round. Doors are framed in and inlaid with antique tile. The roof tiles are larger than often seen and seem to have been produced on site using the traditional method of a worker shaping the still wet clay over his thigh. Many of the tiles have visible fingerprints.

A walled *atrio* (open patio) with a small pool is hidden behind an elaborately painted door seen from the street, while beyond this inner court, under a flying stairway, is the actual front door. At the back of the house, a thick L-shaped

Above: A large wrought iron window grill faces toward the street.

Right: Integrated into a knoll, the house is almost completely merged with the landscape.

Previous pgaes:
Left: Some of the house's many meticulously painted turned balustrades

Middle: The outer entry door, which leads to the forecourt

Right: The second floor cantilevers over the garden.

These pages:
Left: Dramatic arches protruding from either side of the living room fireplace join with the beamed ceiling.

Right: A turned and scrolled banister climbs the stairs in the house's stunning rotunda.

*Below: Typical
equipale guest
seating in the main
courtyard*

*Right: A detail of
the balcony
seemingly held by a
single painted corbel*

colonnade of arches hugs the large inner courtyard. The interior is voluminous and carpeted
in red cement tile. The grand staircase,
accented with more decorative tile, winds up a
mammoth rotunda from which hangs a large
antique casbah lantern. The lush landscaping—
from roses, ferns, and cacti to bougainvillea,
gardenias, and palms—demonstrates that, given
ample water, anything will grow here.

268

Mead House

La Casa de las Campanas, Hancock Park, 1927
Lester Scherer, architect

Lester Scherer remains relatively unknown, but his La Casa de las Campanas, the grand dame of Spanish Colonial houses in Los Angeles, places him among the preeminent architects of the day. Designed in close collaboration with the young Lucile Mead Lamb, daughter of tycoon Willis Howard Mead, the house incorporates a dizzying array of wondrous architectural details. Though its bones are Spanish, there are nods to other styles. An Art Deco flourish is seen in the iron work, especially in the great banister that climbs the stairs in the foyer. The beautiful

Previous pages:
Left: A deeply
carved, eight-
pointed sunburst on
the front door
supported by a motif
suggesting the pipes
of an organ, which
the house has.

Right: The
impressive living
room features some
of the owner's
notable collection of
Californian art.

These pages:
The guest bedroom
features Stickley
beds and other
furnishings original
to the house.

arched cast concrete entryway is of noble
proportion and the cavernous lower rooms
have a Romanesque quality with thick, arched
recesses and halls. Great redwood beams
procured through Mead's company frame the
grand living room. A hulking bell tower anchors
the house to the site and gives the property an
aura of permanence, even as it impresses as a
fantasy realized.

The current owner, who bought the house
and its contents from the Lamb estate, is an
ardent preservationist. He has not only restored
the interiors with the help of interior designer
Rich Assenberg, utilizing the best of the Lamb
collection, but he has also tracked down items
formerly owned by the Mead family and repa-
triated those items throughout the house. The
restoration of this Los Angeles Cultural Heritage Site was ably supported by architects
Tom Michaeli and Barry Milofsky of M2A and
Landscape architect Thomas Cox.

*Above: A tile detail
in the master bath*

*Right: A fountain
surrounded by
mature palms and
native shrubs*

*Following pages:
M2A architects
recreated the
Malibu tile jacuzzi
that cascades into
the pool.*

Overell Estate

La Canada Flintridge, 1929
Lester Scherer and Cyril Bennett, architects

For this house, Scherer partnered again, this time with seasoned Pasadena architect Cyril Bennett. The two collaborated on this dramatic home, built on a huge sloping lot with dramatic views of the San Gabriel Mountains and Alta Canada, for furniture mogul Walter Edward Overell and his wife, Beulah. While Scherer hinted at Deco in his work on La Casa de las Campanas, the Overell estate is a real Art Deco house in the Spanish tradition. Zigzag lines crown Mediterranean arches over the entry and loggias, a style he repeated again the following year on his Church of Our Lady of Lourdes. The effect is something that could be considered very "Hollywood," yet one can picture this house fitting in just as well on the Riviera. The foyer is more open and spare than that of Campanas, but also

Above: A view of the house from the motor court shows a blend of zigzag Art Deco patterns with characteristically Spanish arches and white stucco.

Right: The elaborate cast-concrete entryway

features a towering staircase in the Moderne French style. The abundant stained glass also has a very spare, contemporary quality to it. Most of the generously proportioned rooms are graced with original elaborate light fixtures that incorporate elements of Chinoiserie as well as Art Deco. Likely designed for the house, they are of the type one would have found in the elegant picture houses of the 1920s, some of which Bennett designed. A separate structure houses a four-car garage, uncommon in the day.

The house was meticulously restored by Lauro Guerra and later renovated by designer Mary Serles.

Above: A detail of the mantle

Right: The living room

Above: Peacocks are the theme in the dramatic living room.

Right: Detail of the dining room mantle

*Left: The main
staircase looking up
from the foyer*

*Right: Another
peacock detail from
the dining room,
this time painted on
the ceiling*

*Following pages:
Looking north
toward the
mountains of
Alta Canada*

Villa Primavera
and The Andalusia

West Hollywood, 1923 and 1926
Arthur and Nina Zwebell, architects

The talented, self-taught design-build team of Nina and Arthur Zwebell is responsible for introducing courtyard housing to Los Angeles. This pioneering concept, incorporating multiple dwellings into a single structure centered on a garden, proved to be a hugely popular housing model that continues to be emulated today.

The Zwebells' intuitive understanding of the Spanish Mediterranean building tradition and how it could translate from single family dwelling to multi-family mini communities is evident in their first Spanish Revival courtyard example, Villa Primavera, also known as the Mexican Village. Built in 1923, at a time when there was only one other house in this part of Hollywood, the Zwebells made their home here. The wood and stucco structure wraps around a courtyard with a central fountain and a large outdoor fireplace. The square building contains ten units, most of which are intimate in scale and contain elements that make each apartment feel like a home, including corner fireplaces, recessed nooks and shelves, and Mexican-tile bathrooms and counters. The east wing of the building is two-stories high, with a long balcony overlooking the gardens below. With its rough edges and irregular details, Villa Primavera exudes a more primitive quality than their later work, but the housing ideal achieved by the Zwebells' design is well planned and thoroughly modern.

Having made a name for themselves with Villa Primavera, the Zwebells sold it to finance a new project. More ambitious than Primavera, the Andalusia is their crown jewel and from the start attracted tenants from the Hollywood set including Clara Bow and Cesar Romero. Although at Villa Primavera they did much of the work themselves (the Zwebells were always their own contractors), the Andalusia required the talents of a team of craftsmen.

A view of the courtyard at Villa Primavera, where movie director Nicholas Ray lived while finishing the 1950 noir masterpiece In a Lonely Place, starring Humphrey Bogart. The building was recreated on a sound stage to serve as Bogart's apartment in the film. James Dean and Katherine Hepburn were also residents at one time of the villa.

Following pages:
Left: The large communal fireplace

Right: Interesting details abound, including a faux water jug and a bell dangling above the courtyard

A view of one of the
split-level apartments
at the Andalusia

Right: Another view
of an apartment at the
Andalusia. These were
far more elegant than
those at Villa Primavera.

294

This time, the building was designed around three courtyards: a motor court, a recreation court, and the central main court to which the nine units were oriented. The main court has a central quatrefoil-tiled fountain and a large outdoor fireplace, with semiformal gardens edged by boxwood hedges. These types of courtyard-garden plans create an inviting shared space that fosters a small-village quality all the more appealing today now that a large city has grown around them. This template for designing an oasis in ever-denser urban environments is perhaps the major achievement of the Zwebell courts.

Above: Detail of the fountain at Villa Primavera

Right: Looking through an arch into the courtyard at the Andalusia

The Rindge/Adamson Legacy

Bostonian Frederick Hastings Rindge and his wife, May Knight Rindge, purchased the 13,330-acre Malibu Rancho in 1892. This now-famous stretch of rolling hills along the Pacific Ocean served as the Rindge ranch, where they raised cattle and grain. The grounds eventually grew to 17,000 acres and was one of the most valuable privately-held pieces of property in the United States. When Rindge died at the age of 48 in 1905, his wife took over as steward of the family holdings. In 1924, she built Malibu Dam, and, in 1928, began construction of what was to be a 50-room castle, a massive undertaking that she oversaw until her death in 1941, but which sadly never saw completion. However, the house she planned for her daughter, Rhoda Rindge Adamson and her new husband, Merritt, on a hill overlooking the Malibu lagoon was built and remains a local landmark.

From both financial and logistical necessity, May Rindge founded the Malibu Potteries. She needed tile and other building materials for her houses, but also sold tile to contractors around Southern California, where they found their way into the many civic structures rising up around Los Angeles as well as fine houses all over. These tiles, with their distinctive patterns gleaned mainly from North Africa, Spain, and Mexico, have become iconic details identified with the great age of American Spanish Colonial Revival architecture and are treasured today.

The 1930s presented unprecedented challenges to the Rindge legacy. Along with great financial strain brought on by the Depression, the potteries were lost to fire and never rebuilt, and her private coastal Eden was opened to the public, who had fought for and won the right to build a highway through her property. The ranch was eventually parceled off, and the remaining 26 acres surrounding her unfinished castle were sold to the Franciscan order. It is now known as the Junipero Serra retreat.

Right: The original Adamson House in Hancock Park as it is today

Following pages: Left: Iron griffons over the banister

Middle: Looking through iron gates opening to the original porte-cochere

Right: Tile and terra cotta from the Malibu Potteries in the courtyard seating area and balcony of the guest house.

The great room of the Adamson House at Hancock Park, shown here, foreshadows the grandeur of the Adamson House in Malibu (shown on following pages).

Adamson House

Hancock Park, 1922
Elmer Grey, architect

In the 1920s, Rhoda Rindge Adamson with her husband Merritt Adamson, first captain of the University of Southern California Trojans and a former employee of her father's, lived in this house designed by architect Elmer Grey in Hancock Park. They had become a successful couple on their own, their Adohr Farms (Adohr being Rhoda spelled backwards), located in the nearby San Fernando Valley, having become one of the largest milk producers in the world.

The house was a standard Italianate Mediterranean that subsequent owners have reworked into more Monterey Spanish by removing the ornate Renaissance-revival door frame and adding a long second-story balcony. It is now a more fitting home for the Malibu terra-cotta and tile work found in and around the house. The game room downstairs is reminiscent of the beach house hall (right), though with a brick-tile floor instead of a faux Persian rug. There is an especially interesting fountain under the guest house balcony, which is supported by red terra-cotta columns also produced at Malibu. The current owners have restored the house and gardens with the help of restoration architects Mary Pickhardt, Bebe Johnson, and Ellen Geerer.

Adamson House

Malibu, 1930
Morgan, Walls, and Clements, architects

The second Adamson house, planned by Rhoda's mother, May Rindge, for Malibu Lagoon's Vaquero Point, was realized in 1930. Architect Stiles O. Clements of the venerable firm Morgan, Walls, and Clements delivered more than the average beach house for the young couple. A blend of Andalusian Spanish and Moorish architecture, the house is the perfect backdrop for the tile art that frames recessed windows and doors and forms murals and a large reproduction Persian rug. Clements incorporated hand-carved teak doors, murals by Ejnar Hansen and Peter Nielsen, molded ceilings, filigree ironwork, and bottle glass windows.

The entry court leads to a deep-set door featuring panels made up of round bottle bottoms set under a stone arch emulating rays of light. The outside patios, pathways, and fountains are all further celebrations of the Malibu Potteries creations. The central court facing the lagoon is flanked on either side by wings that have a subtle, flat, zigzag roofline. The courtyard is framed to the west by the iconic and much copied peacock wall fountain. Other courtyards

Above: The entry approach from the motor court

Right: The front facade facing toward the lagoon

Following pages: Left: An outdoor corner fireplace next to a tiled door surround

Middle: The living room's donkey window, so named after passageways in northern Africa designed to accommodate wide loads and a rider

Right: The arch over the front door emulates beams of light.

and circular garden areas around the property are reinforced by impressive rustic brick and stonework. Not to be overlooked is the beautiful flat-roofed hacienda-style pool house featuring an inset central porch where one will find Hansen and Nielsen's famed Portola Mural over the fireplace.

Today, the Adamson House is a National Historic Site and the jewel of the California State Parks system.

Above: The hall with its Persian-inspired tile carpet

Right: The well-worn chair and smoke stained patina throughout the room remind us that this was once a well lived in home.

Following pages: The famous Adamson peacock fountain

Morgan House

Los Angeles, 1929
Morgan, Walls and Clements, architects

Stiles Clements designed this traditional Spanish courtyard–style house for his partner and friend, Octavius Morgan. It was completed around the same time as the Adamson house in Malibu. The two architects had had a hand in designing some of the most elaborate churrigueresque picture palaces along the Broadway theater district but took a more sober approach to the design of this house.

Located right in the middle of Los Angeles' Miracle Mile neighborhood off of Wilshire Boulevard near the La Brea Tar Pits, this house is a perfectly scaled Spanish courtyard home with a few surprises. Understated from the street, undulating yet smooth stucco walls give little away about the house's actual layout. A very low pitched tile roof extends along the south facade, which hides the home's main courtyard and also covers the deceivingly large sunken living room that allows for a near double-height ceiling. The house has a formal

Above: The bottle-glass window off the hall opens into the living room.

Right: The sunken living room of the single-story house is illuminated in part thanks to the clever slanting of its small windows.

Previous pages:
Left: Stenciled leather
arches in the hall

Middle: Another
view of the hall
looking toward the
living room

Right: View toward
dining room and its
dyed, scored plaster
ceiling

dining room, library, and large living room, as well as a master bedroom that opens up to its own secondary courtyard. Surprisingly, there is not much tile, but the house shares other elements with the Adamson beach house, including scored plaster ceilings, deep set windows designed to give the illusion of an adobe built structure, and numerous stenciled walls and ceilings.

The house and gardens were meticulously restored by architectural preservationist Brett Watermann.

Above: The main courtyard and pool

Right: The arched wood-burning stove off the main courtyard

Keeler House

South Gate, 1926
Rufus Keeler, architect

Rufus Keeler was the founder, manager, and sole ceramicist of both the Malibu and Calco potteries. Under his direction, in the 1920s and 30s, the two companies produced the finest tile art ever made in Southern California.

Keeler was not a wealthy man, but he loved his art. He built himself what he described as an "everyday home" in the southern Los Angeles suburb of South Gate, not far from Watts. The small house boasts an important collection of Calco and Malibu tile art. Adamson house docents have referred to Keeler's house as the "little Adamson House." The current owner begs to differ, insisting that a more accurate title is the "father of the Adamson House."

The house was designed around a courtyard, with the master bedroom, dining room, and music room all opening onto a patio with a round pool and fountain. To one side is a

Above: A tile mural under the living room windows

Right: A pathway leading to the entrance

Following pages: Left: The front door with a river-of-life motif and rustic Calco-tile surround

Middle: View through an arched doorway from the dining room

Right: Tile wainscoting and border detail.

sleeping porch with beds that fold out from the wall. Among its more impressive features are a squeeze-bag tile mural Keeler made in the nearby city of Vernon copied from a Tunisian carpet pattern that is the height of the house and the nine-foot tall Calco Mayan fireplace modeled after the Temple of the Cross in Palenque, Mexico.

Every piece of hardware was hand wrought by an Italian blacksmith named Clementino Lombardo, who built his forge in the front yard. Working with Keeler on the designs, they created beautiful door screens, light fixtures, and other elements, all still intact.

It is worth noting that Simon Rodia worked for Keeler at Calco, and he decorated his famed Watts Towers nearby with damaged tiles from there and the Malibu Potteries.

Above: The living room

Right: The library

Following pages: Left: Mantle detail

Middle: The unique Calco fireplace, modeled after a Mayan temple in Palenque

Right: Mantle detail

Above: A patio wall fountain, one of a number of details unchanged since the house was photographed for Rexford Newcomb's 1928 book, Mediterranean Domestic Architecture in the United States.

Right: The shady courtyard

Following pages: Tile detail

The inviting facade of this Beverly Hills bungalow

Following pages: California antiques, including a Catalina oil jar on the hearth, are found in the living room.

A Collector's Home

Beverly Hills, 1927
Architect unknown

The owner of this house and its remarkable collection truly loves Los Angeles and its rich heritage. This two-story Spanish-style bungalow tucked in a canyon in Beverly Hills and set amongst palm and citrus trees does not give much away from the street except its unusual Claycraft tile. The architect is not known, but it is likely that, like so many of these houses, it was contractor built based on any number of plan books used at the time. Passing through the front door, one enters an amazing world of tile vignettes that celebrate the historic roots of the southwest and evoke the romance of 1920s California. Images of galleons, old missions, Spanish dancers, and tropical birds fill nooks, decorate walls, and cover table tops. Grouped by theme, from the "Mission Room" to the "Tijuana Hotel Room," the space reads like a museum. The fabulous collection includes vintage Monterey furniture, California pottery, and rare tile from the Malibu and Catalina

potteries, among others. In the courtyard, a potted garden of agaves, cacti, and other desert bloomers fills the space topped off by a sleeping Mexican figure.

The owner began collecting 25 years ago, after visiting the Adamson house in Malibu and becoming inspired by the beauty of the tile. It became a life-long pursuit that ultimately led her to become an Adamson House docent and board member helping to promote and preserve the house and its legacy for future generations.

Above: Between two Monterey wing back chairs sits a Malibu ship tile table in original iron.

Right: Malibu and D&M ship tiles mounted on the walls of the living room

Previous pages:
The dining room,
complete with an
imperial sideboard
inset with Malibu
tiles

These pages:
Left: San Jose Tile
Workshop tile light
fixture sconce of
woman carrying
water through her
Mexican village

Right: Bauer
Ringware coffee
server set atop a
rare Malibu tile-
top table resting on
a Coronado leather
top hexagon table

Far right:
Coronado hutch
filled with beautiful
pottery and tiles
from Catalina,
Malibu, Pacific,
Bauer, Tudor, and
Taylor potteries.
The tile on the left
bottom is a fringe
tile from the
famous Adamson
House rug.

Above: The guest bathroom

Right: The guest bedroom has a cowboy theme with a framed print of Will Rogers. The wall mirror is Monterey style. The decorative painting by Gloria Fisher is titled The Old California Store.

342

*Left: The homeowner
has decorated her yard
with vintage garden
ornamentation,
including birdbaths
and garden pots that
are planted with
succulents and cactus.*

Right: A garden detail

Casa Salchicha

Santa Ynez, 2001
Jeff Gorrell/Lenvick & Minor, architect

The influence of the Adamson's Malibu beach house is celebrated in this contemporary house designed and built by its owners as a labor of love. In so many ways, it exemplifies the right way to recreate a period revival house that can feel as timeless as one built in the 1920s. Though not a copy of the original, many of the house's elements, from the Persian rug and basket weave floor tile patterns to the pointed arch of the dining room's donkey window, pay homage to the greatness achieved by Stiles Clements' design.

While some of the tile is old, most is styled after that of the Adamson House and made by Richard Keit and Mary Kennedy of RTK Studios in Ojai, California. All of the light fixtures and door handles in the house are antique pieces from homes of the 1920s. There are

Above: A sausage on a skewer crowns the house.

Right: A broad view of the approach. The roof tiles are stacked and boosted as much as five high.

stained glass panels from the original Tiffany Studios as well as stained Norman slab glass made by the fifth-generation Judson Studios of Highland Park, California, Judson Studios having also made glass for the Adamson house.

Through their research, the owners were guided by traditional mythology about Spanish homes. One myth, for example, prompted them to incorporate broken tile into the entry and fireplace because evil spirits cannot travel through broken lines. Deliberate inconsistencies were also incorporated, such as different door handles on all the doors and varied ceiling heights since, as it is said, "houses were not meant to be perfect because the only perfect thing is God."

Above: In the library, a late 1880s original Tiffany window depicts the subject of its title, William the Conqueror of 1066.

Right: The kitchen. The tile seen throughout the house is custom made by Richard Keit and Mary Kennedy of RTK tile in Ojai.

Following pages: The covered patio looks out to a bucolic equestrian setting.

Pages 356–57: One of many fountains inspired by the Adamson House in Malibu

Acknowledgments

Thank you to our publisher, Charles Miers, and our editors, David Morton and Douglas Curran, for their thoughtful encouragement, considered criticism, and most of all, your faith in us. Thanks as well to Abigail Sturges, for putting it all together so beautifully.

Much gratitude goes out to all of the homeowners for opening their doors to us; we could not have done this without them.

DW ML

We also wish to thank the following friends for helping in so many ways.

Crosby Doe
Barry Sloan
Harry Kolbe
Christi Walden
Brett Watermann
Rosemary Connelly and the Coda family
Craig Wright
Dirk Sutro
Diane Wilk
Michael Burch
Raun Thorp
Liz Page
Liv Ballard
Brian Kaiser
Erik Evans
Marc Appleton
John McIntyre
Michael Berger
The Yust family
Allegra, Lauren and Christopher

Bibliography

Ames, Meriam. *Rancho Santa Fe: A California Village*. San Diego, CA: Rancho Santa Fe Historical Society, 1995.

Appleton, Marc. *George Washington Smith: An Architect's Scrapbook*. Los Angeles, CA: Tailwater Press, 2001.

——. with Melba Levick. *California Mediterranean*. New York: Rizzoli, 2007.

Baxter Art Gallery. *Caltech, 1910–1950: An Urban Architecture for Southern California*. Pasadena, CA: Caltech, 1983.

——. *Myron Hunt, 1868–1952. The Search for Regional Architecture*. Santa Monica, CA: Hennessey & Ingalls, 1984

Bottomley, William Lawrence. *Spanish Details*. New York: W. Helburn, Inc., 1924.

Bricker, Lauren Weiss. *Johnson, Kaufmann, Coate; Partners in the California Style*. Claremont, CA: Scripps College, 1992.

Byne, Arthur and Mildred Stapley. *Majorcan Houses and Gardens: A Spanish Island in the Mediterranean*. New York: William Helburn, 1928.

——. *Spanish Gardens and Patios*. Philadelphia, PA: J. B. Lippincott, 1924.

——. *Spanish Interiors and Furniture*. New York: William Helburn, 1925.

——. *Spanish Ironwork*. New York: Hispanic Society, 1915.

Gebhard, David & Robert Winter. *1868–1968, Architecture in California*. Santa Barbara, CA: UCSB, 1968.

——. *A Guide to Architecture in Los Angeles Southern California*. Layton, UT: Peregrine Smith. 1977.

——. *Los Angeles: An Architectural Guide*. Salt Lake City, UT. 1994

Gebhard, Patricia. *George Washington Smith: Architect of the Spanish-Colonial Revival*. Layton, UT: Gibbs Smith, 2005.

Greenberg, David and Kathryn Smith. *Malibu Tile*. Los Angeles, CA: Craft and Folk Art Museum, 1980.

Hannaford, Donald R. and Revel Edwards. *Spanish Colonial or Adobe Architecture of California*. New York: Architectural Book Publishing Co., 1931.

Hess, Alan. *Rancho Deluxe: Rustic Dreams and Real Western Living*. San Francisco, CA. Chronicle Books, 2000.

Hines, Thomas, S. *Irving Gill and the Architecture of Reform: A Study in Modernist Architectural Culture*. New York. Monacelli Press, 2000.

Hudson, Karen. *Paul R. Williams: A Legacy of Style*. New York: Rizzoli, 1993.

Hunter, Paul Robinson, and Walter L. Reichardt. *Residential Architecture in Southern California*. AIA, 1939. Santa Monica, CA: Hennessey & Ingalls, reprinted, 1998.

Kanner, Diane. *Wallace Neff and the Grand Houses of the Golden State*. New York: Monacelli Pres, 2005.

Lamb, Lucile Mead. *". . . Tells of Her Adventures in Homebuilding."* Los Angeles. Themus, Zeta Tau Alpha, 1929.

McMillian, Elizabeth. *California Colonial: The Spanish and Rancho Revival Styles* (Schiffer Design Book). Atglen, PA: Schiffer Publishing, 2002.

——. with Melba Levick. *Casa California: Spanish-Style Houses from Santa Barbara to San Clemente*. New York: Rizzoli, 1996.

Michaud, Roland and Sabrina with Michael Barry. *Design and Color in Islamic Architecture: Eight Centuries of the Tile-Maker's Art*. New York: Vendome, 1996.

Neff, Jr., Wallace (ed.), David Gebhard, Alson Clark, Wallace Neff. *Wallace Neff: Architect of California's Golden Age*. Santa Monica, CA: Hennessey & Ingalls, 2000.

Neff, Wallace. *Wallace Neff (1895–1982): The Romance of Regional Architecture*. Huntington Library, 1989. Santa Monica, CA: Hennessey & Ingalls, Reprinted 1998.

Newcomb, Rexford. *Franciscan Mission Architecture in Alta California*. New York: Architectural Book Publishing Company, 1916.

——. *Old Mission Churches and Historic Houses of California*. Philadelphia, PA: J. B. Lippincott, 1925.

——. *The Spanish House for America: It's Design, Furnishing and Garden*. Philadelphia, PA: J. B. Lippincott, 1927.

——. *Spanish-Colonial Architecture in the United States*. New York: J. J. Augustin, 1937.

——. *Mediterranean Domestic Architecture for the United States*, (Acanthus Press Reprint Series). New York: Acanthus Press, 1999.

Ovnick, Merry. *Los Angeles: The End of the Rainbow*. Los Angeles, CA: Balcony Press, 1994.

Paccard, Andre. *Traditional Islamic Craft in Moroccan Architecture*. Paris: Atilier 74, 1980.

Peuriot, Francoise. *Arabesques: Decorative Art in Morocco*. Paris: ACR, 1999.

Polyzoides, Stefanos, Roger Sherwood, James Tice. *Courtyard Housing in Los Angeles: A Typological Analysis*. New York: Princeton Architectural Press, 1997.

Poole, Jean and Tevvy Ball. *El Pueblo: The Historic Heart of Los Angeles*. Los Angeles, CA: Getty Trust Publications, 2002.

Requa, Richard. *Architectural Details: Spain and the Mediterranean*. Cleveland, OH: J. H. Jansen, 1927.

——. *Old World Inspiration for American Architecture*. Denver, CO: Monolith Portland Midwest Company, 1929.

Rindge, Frederick H. *Happy Days in Southern California*. Cambridge, MA: Knickerbocker, 1898.

Soule, Winsor. *Spanish Farm Houses and Minor Public Buildings*. New York: Architectural Book Publishing Company, 1924.

Sweeney, Robert, Marc Walla and Marc Appleton. *Casa del Herrero: The Romance of Spanish Colonial*. New York: Rizzoli, 2009.

Watters, Sam. *Los Angeles Houses 1885–1919*. New York: Acanthus, 2007

——. *Los Angeles Houses 1920–1935*. New York: Acanthus, 2007

Weitze, Karen. *California's Mission Revival*. Santa Monica, CA: Hennessey + Ingalls, 1984.

Williams, Greg. *The Story of Hollywoodland*. Hollywood, CA: Papavasilopoulos Press, 1992.

Winslow, Carleton and Clarence Stein. *Gardens of the San Diego Exposition*. San Francisco, CA: Elder, 1916.

Wyllie, Romy. *Bertram Goodhue: His Life And Residential Architecture*. New York: W. W. Norton, 2007.

Index